Forex Trading

Ultimate Proven Guide to Profitable Trading

(Volume I - Introduction to the markets)

Josh Bright

© **Copyright Josh Bright 2018 - All rights reserved.**

The contents of this book may not be reproduced, duplicated or transmitted without direct written permission from the author.

Under no circumstances will any legal responsibility or blame be held against the publisher for any reparation, damages, or monetary loss due to the information herein, either directly or indirectly.

Legal Notice:

This book is copyright protected. This is only for personal use. You cannot amend, distribute, sell, use, quote or paraphrase any part of the content of this book without the consent of the author.

Disclaimer Notice:

Please note the information contained in this document is for educational and entertainment purposes only. Every attempt has been made to provide accurate, up to date and complete, reliable information. No warranties of any kind are expressed or implied. Readers acknowledge that the author is not engaging in the rendering of legal, financial, medical or professional advice. The content of this book has been derived from various sources. Please consult a licensed professional before attempting any techniques outlined in this book.

By reading this document, the reader agrees that under no circumstances are the author responsible for any losses, direct or indirect, which are incurred as a result of the use of information contained within this document, including, but not limited to, —errors, omissions, or inaccuracies."

Table of Contents

Chapter 1: Introducing Financial Markets 1

Chapter 2: What Is Online Trading 7

Chapter 3: How To Make Money Trading 11

Chapter 4: Different Markets To Consider When Trading .. 16

Chapter 5: Technical Analysis When Trading Financial Markets 20

Chapter 6: Fundamental Analysis and How To Use It 25

Chapter 7: What Is a Trend and How To Ride It 30

Chapter 8: Classic Technical Analysis Patterns To Use In Any Market 33

Chapter 9: Elliott Waves Theory and Why Traders Love It 37

Chapter 10: The Japanese Approach To Technical Analysis 42

Chapter 11: The Most Important Economic News That Matters 49

Chapter 12: Central Banks and Their Role in Financial Markets 54

Chapter 13: Market Psychology And Why Knowing Yourself Matters The Most 59

Chapter 14: Introduction to Money Management 63

Chapter 15: Different Trading Styles 66

Chapter 1

Introducing Financial Markets

Financial markets represent the place where traders around the world buy and sell a security. Be it stocks, currencies, bonds, options, indices, etc., the term financial markets refers to any financial product that can be traded.

People that buy and sell financial products for a profit are traders. A trader, in essence, is a speculator.

The game of speculation existed before the notion of trading financial markets appeared. Since money appeared, people had different ideas about the value of a product. Because valuation changes based on perception, goods are perceived as having different value by different people.

But what is money and why do we need money for our society to function? Before anything, the starting point when referring to money is trust.

If there's no trust between the two parties in a transaction, the transaction doesn't take place. But, the belief doesn't refer to the two parties' faith in each other, but the trust in the vehicle that intermediates the transaction. Or, in the money.

In time, money took various shapes and forms. Nowadays we talk about banknotes, electronic money and even virtual currencies (crypto).

 Back in time, trading starting with exchanging  goods for something else people needed. For example, the butcher in a community traded the meet with the brewer. Hence, one got the beer and the other the meat. That's trading in its most incipient form. That's barter.

The closest form of today's money was the coins. Rulers imposed Gold, silver and copper coins and they circulated for a long time throughout vast empires.

Modern central banks set the monetary policy for a currency using the interest rate level to stem inflation. However, the monetary policy or how to influence the value of a currency is as old as gold and silver coins.

Monarchs and emperors decided to increase or decrease the percentage of gold in gold coins, thus influencing their value. Have you  ever watched a movie to see people effectively bite a gold coin?

That's because they don't trust the money. A healthy bite would tell you if that's real gold or the gold is only at the surface.

Speaking of gold, to this day it is considered the closest form of money that ever existed. The reason comes from the fact that over five thousand years gold fascinated humankind. Moreover, it was part of every kind of transactions one can imagine.

The modern financial system derives from gold too. After coins became so popular, people realized it is difficult to conduct financial transactions due to their weight.

When Italian merchants from Venice, Florence, and Genova started establishing "branches" in foreign territories, they issued the first form of banknotes as we are known them today. Against a piece of paper (or what was then paper), one could step into a branch and receive the amount of gold needed.

Hence, no need to travel with the money, the danger of being robbed disappeared, and commercial banking was born.

Fast forward to modern central banking, the Riksbank in Sweden, the oldest central bank in the world, was the first one to issue banknotes. They were so good that people trusted they'll receive the amount of gold from the bank by merely showing up with the notes.

However, the bank issued more banknotes than the gold it owned, causing a massive loss of trust among the banknotes holders. It was the first time a bank defaulted, and to this day when trust is lost, money loses value or even disappears.

During the World War I, and after, central banks had a big role in stabilizing the devastating economies. It was the age of famous central bankers like Montagu Norman at the Bank of England, Emile Moreau of Banque de France, Schacht in Germany and the incomparable head of the Federal Reserve of the United States, Benjamin Strong.

The amount of gold held by the banks dictated the power and influence in any negotiation between the big powerhouses.

Monetary policy was conducted considering the value of money and the perception among the population.

When Germany was asked to pay for war reparations, it realized it didn't have the money (a.k.a. gold) and will loan the nation's future by accepting the Allies' terms. It was already from that moment that the unrest started to build and the seeds for the World War II were planted.

The 1944 Bretton Woods agreement put a new order in the world's financial system. Ravaged by war, Europe and Japan, couldn't argue with the leading role of the U.S. Dollar.

It became the "de-facto" world's reserve currency, with the Federal Reserve of the United States taking the role of the leader of modern banking. However, the U.S. Dollar was backed by gold, and that was a comfort for other countries.

But the Nixon administration decided in 1971 to scrap the gold standard, as it couldn't finance the enormous deficits that started to build. The whole world watched scared to see if the trust will break.

Remember what makes money? Trust!

As it turned out, they trusted the Fed and the U.S. Dollar and the rest, as we know, is history.

2018 modern central banking evolved into sophisticated practices to stimulate inflation and the economic development all around the world. But one thing didn't change: the desire of people to speculate on the value of money, as well as the power it brings.

"Let me issue and control a nation's money and I care not who writes the laws" – Mayer Amschel Rothschild (1744-1812), the founder of the House of Rothschild.

Chapter 2

What Is Online Trading

Since the Personal Computer's invention in 1975, financial trading changed for good. Suddenly, computer power is used for charting, documenting patterns, building technical indicators, etc.

The world changed since the PC's invention, and trading changed too. In the early 90's another breakthrough changed our societies forever: The Internet.

By that time, new generations of PC's showed the power of computing, and traders didn't have to write down the price of a stock to build a chart anymore. Instead, merely putting the numbers in a computer program will result in the PC "spitting" the desired chart.

The first lines written in the HTML language forever changed the world. The Internet disrupted industries buried  many businesses and opened the potential for entirely new products.

Online financial trading is just one of them. Until the Internet, financial trading took a lot of time. Traders needed to step into a brokerage house (or give a phone call), instruct the clerk to buy some stocks, the clerk would run to the counter, shout the order, wait for confirmation, and so on. By the time the answer came, the market may have moved a few points already.

But the most significant change came from another direction. The Internet gave access to a whole new class of traders to the financial markets: the retail traders.

In the United States investing in the stock market was popular among retail traders anyways. But the rest of the world lacked that American entrepreneurial instinct of risking a lot on the stock market.

With online access, brokers spotted the opportunity of bringing the market to everyone's attention. Not only that anyone with an Internet connection can actively trade, but new industries appeared. Such an industry turned out to be the largest financial market in the world: Foreign Exchange or Forex.

The truth is that the market already existed. The interbank market is the "playground" where commercial banks exchange a currency against another.

Speculators from all corners of the world bet against a currency or bought another one mainly for fundamental reasons. Big investment houses in the United States had clerks waking up in the morning to check up prices in Asia and ask the local trading desk to buy or sell currencies.

But accessing the interbank market was an expensive product. Retail traders didn't have the resources nor the infrastructure to participate in "the trading game." As such, it remained for years a "big boys" arena, with very few individuals taking part in currency market speculation.

The Internet changed that. Brokers spotted the opportunity and started online businesses, offering traders the possibility of taking part of the most extensive financial market in the world.

Obviously, against a fee or commission. But the progress existed, and with little capital traders could access the interbank market, having the broker as the middleman.

Online trading started having difficult times, but that changed as the Internet gained more and more fans and trading became more and more  popular. Not to mention that technology changed so much that today's Personal Computers, smartphones, 4G networks, etc., made it possible to trade virtually any financial product around the world, from the comfort of your own house.

All you need is stable Internet. And, of course, some money in the trading account.

Chapter 3

How To Make Money Trading

Trading financial markets started with the stock market in the United States. A trader speculates on the future direction of a stock, to make a profit.

In time, other products became available for trading, like currencies, bonds, options, futures, derivates, funds, indexes, and so on. The list is so big that it doesn't worth mentioning every market here.

But the trading principle is the same. Pick a market, whatever that is, and you feel comfortable trading it, and decide if the price will go up or down. That's it! You're in the trading business!

What can be so tricky? After all, it's a fifty-fifty chance to be right or wrong.

The art of speculation is called an "art" for a reason. Trading is not gambling, and this is not a video game.

Instead, the sudden changes in prices you see when looking at the stock market or the currency market, represent the result of real people buying and selling. It is a dog eat dog world that will eat you alive if you're not ready for it.

The idea of these books is to create a mindset for the individual trader to make it in the world's financial markets. Moreover, to build a framework and an understanding of what trading is and how to become successful in trading. Or, how to make money trading!

When you like something in the financial world, like a stock or a currency pair or even the way the economy performs, you're BULLISH. You want to buy or go LONG.

The term has an exciting root as it comes from the horns of a bull, always pointing to the upside. It is no wonder it became the Wall Street symbol everyone knows today!

Hence, traders go long when they buy financial security. How about going SHORT?

The opposite of buying, going short means traders grow BEARISH. To express the bearishness, they sell a financial product or market.

Still, an animal sits at the origin of this financial term: the bears. As it walks with the head always pointing to the ground, it became the image of traders that want to go short or sell something.

For this reason, traders often refer to trading as a battle between bulls and bears, a bull/bear fight that in the end will move the market.

Bullish and bearish is the equivalent of HAWKISH and DOVISH. Central bankers may have a hawkish statement about the future of the economy, which translates into being bullish for traders.

The term comes from the hawk in the sky, which flies at higher altitudes. The opposite, the dove, flies lower and has bearish implications for financial traders.

Quite many animals in the trading world's terminology, isn't it?

When you grow bullish and buy a security, the only way to make a profit (or money) is if the security's price rises. Think of gold reaching $2000? Buy it now when it trades $1327!

For what is worth, XAUUSD is the financial name for gold, and the two prices represent the bid and ask prices. In our next book part of this series dedicated to how to make it in the financial markets, we'll deal with everything that goes into a trading account.

Coming back to our example, if gold goes move to $2000, the difference represents the profit: $2000-$1327=$673. Not bad for a trade!

But things go a bit more complicated than that. The volume traded matters too. Typically, gold will take a lot of time to travel such a distance, but that doesn't mean a profit like this can't be made on smaller moves. Increasing the trading volume will do the trick, but the risk becomes bigger too.

If a trader believes the U.S. Dollar will lose value against the Euro, due to changes in the macroeconomic picture, etc., he/she will sell short the EURUSD pair. If the pair drops, a profit is made. If not, the trading account takes a loss.

Success in financial markets doesn't mean a string of winning trades only. That's one of the biggest misperceptions retail traders have: they just want to win.

That's impossible, as there's no holy grail in trading. Instead, learn to embrace losses as part of the trading game, and focus on having more winning than losing trades.

As such, the trading account will grow, leading to financial success. More on that, on the part where we will deal with trading psychology and money management.

Chapter 4

Different Markets To Consider When Trading

The beauty in financial markets is that they trade pretty much the same way. With a few exceptions (e.g., options), traders focus on the direction (long or short) and the money management to achieve the result with as little damage as possible.

However, different markets have their particularities worth considering, like:

- **Forex.** Forex comes from the foreign exchange market, and we'll focus on it on our next book in this series. On the Forex market, traders from all corners of the world meet to buy and sell currency pairs (not currencies!). Against a commission/fee, plenty of brokers give access to the interbank market, offering different types of trading accounts in the process.

- **Stock Market**. Trading the stock market depends on what the objective is. One can trade individual stocks or an index.  Moreover, with the emergence of ETF's (Exchange Traded Funds), there are a plethora of opportunities to take advantage of the stock market moves.

- **Options Market**. Not to be confused with the binary market, the real options market is highly traded in the United States of America. Traders use sophisticated methods to speculate on call and put options for every possible financial product. The expiration date for these options profoundly influences the volatility in related markets (e.g., when huge options expire on the currency market, the volatility around fixings experiences great levels, making it difficult to trade Forex).

- **Other Markets**. The general name here is well-intended as the markets that fit this category aren't so popular among retail traders, with one exception: CFD's. Since their introduction, Contracts for Difference allow traders to speculate on virtually any market: commodities, indices, individual stocks, etc. As always, there's a catch: higher commissioning and margin needed for a trade. However, besides CFD's, interesting financial markets are:

- Futures
- Futures Options
- Warrants
- Metals
- Single Stock Futures (SSF's)
- Structured Products
- Bonds
- Funds

By this time, it should be clear that financial markets are quite a complicated arena, with buyers and sellers meeting with one and only one intention: to make a profit.

Depending on the trading style (we'll cover later in this book different approaches to the market), some are more aggressive or conservative than others. The best part of it is that current brokers offer access to more than one single market.

For example, Forex brokers offer not only access to the interbank currency market but also to precious metals, individual stocks, and indices, bonds, etc. All via CFD's products.

Being able to access different markets help savvy traders in diversifying the risk in a trading account. After all, the first thing to consider when trading is how to manage the risk (or how NOT to lose) before looking at how much you'll make.

Because markets experience different correlations, both intra- and inter-market, there's a fine line between diversification and overtrading. At the end of this books series, you'll be able to tell that on your own.

CHAPTER 5

Technical Analysis When Trading Financial Markets

Technical analysis is as old as charting. Since traders were able to build a chart, they started draw trend lines, document patterns, and even create trading theories based on the correlation between market sentiment and human nature (e.g., Elliott Waves Theory).

The art of interpreting a chart represents technical analysis. Historical prices offer a clue over what might happen with future prices.

Any trader know uses technical analysis concepts to find places where the market might turn. Even traders that base their analysis on macroeconomic aspects look at primary trendlines and apply basic technical analysis concepts to more significant timeframes.

The area of technical analysis is so vast and complex; it deserves a particular book in our series. As a matter of fact, we'll treat most of the technical concepts available in today's markets not only in one book but in several, going into details from describing the idea to the actual implementation.

Technical analysis changed in time as the tools to approach the market evolved. At first, traders used pen and paper to record the movements of a financial product.

Next, after the PC appeared, charting became easier. It was during the 1980's when main technical analysis indicators appeared, as traders found it easier to compile the data with the help of computers.

Today's technical traders use:

- **Technical Analysis Tools**. A set of technical tools that differs from trading platform to trading platform, that mainly consists of:
- Fibonacci tools – retracement, fan, expansion, time zones, arcs
- Gann tools – grid, line, fan
- Trendlines
- Channels
- Shapes to measure the time
- Pitchforks
- Angles

- Chart types – candlesticks, line, bars
- Market geometry
- Classic chart patterns

- **Indicators**. A favorite way for traders to ride trends or to pick tops and bottoms, indicators split into:

    - Trend indicators – they follow the trend helping traders to buy dips in bullish trends and sell spikes in bearish ones.

    - Oscillators – indicators placed at the bottom of a chart, that help traders spotting fake moves. Either buying oversold and selling overbought areas, or even trading bullish or bearish divergences, traders like oscillators as they help to pick significant tops and bottoms.

- **Trading Theories**. A trading theory offers a comprehensive analysis of an entire market. Thus, not only that it gives a possible trade, but an understanding of where the market comes from and where it'll go. Most representative trading theories are:

- Elliott Waves Theory
- Dow Theory
- Gartley
- Gann
- Harmonics
- Point and Figure
- Drummond
- Japanese Candlesticks Techniques

Again, these are only some of the trading theories, indicators, and basic tools to use in technical analysis. The idea was to bring in front of you some of the ways used by technical traders to understand how the market moves.

Some firmly believe they work. However, to this day there's no holy grail in technical trading, in the sense that there's no one tool or theory that gives a hundred percent winning trades.

But they do help traders finding better entries, filtering fake moves, and making better trading decisions overall.

Those that don't believe in technical analysis turn to fundamental. If the technical analysis offers the direction, the fundamental analysis deals with the reason why the market moves.

Chapter 6

Fundamental Analysis and How To Use It

The sum of everything that influences the price of a financial security or product represents fundamental analysis. Most think of fundamental analysis as only economic news. That's wrong.

Everything else matters. For example:

- An oil pipeline explodes in Nigeria, disrupting the oil flow to major African ports: that's bullish oil as it influences demand and bullish CAD (Canadian Dollar) as the oil and CAD enjoy a direct correlation.

- Hurricanes impacts the United States economy, thus influencing the Fed's monetary policy decisions

- European Central Bank (ECB) decides to end the Quantitative Easing (QE) program, thus making the Euro more attractive to investors.

Obviously, these are only some stories that create volatility in financial markets. Along those lines, think of anything that might impact the market you're in, and that's part of fundamental analysis.

However, most of the times the economic news is the fundamental reason behind a market's move. Be it stocks, options, or currency, the economic news lead traders to forming an idea about the shape of an economy, and what the central bank will do with the interest rates next.

The economic news comes out in a structured fashion. Due to the economic calendar, which is free information for every market participant to know, traders know in advance what the next piece of economic data will be. And, its impact.

In financial markets, the central role belongs to central banks. Modern central banking made financial markets dependent on the interest rate level and the monetary policy engaged by major central banks.

Thus, traders use the economic calendar and interpret the news to form an idea about what the central bank will do next: will it raise, lower, or keep the interest rate unchanged.

Sometimes economic news becomes secondary. Because other events dominate the headline, even medium-term trading scraps economic news.

The best example comes from the year 2016. The United Kingdom voted in a historic referendum, deciding the leave the European Union.

However, the vote took place in June. Or, over five months into the 2016 trading year.

All that time before the vote, the currency market, for example, didn't go anywhere. Regardless how many times the GDP (Gross Domestic Product) was released, or NFP (Non-Farm Payrolls) in the United States, no currency pairs went anywhere.

Moreover, even the Brexit referendum wasn't enough to wake up markets from their dull trading. How come?

The focus then shifted to the U.S. Presidential elections. As the polls suggested a tight race (and it was a tight one), financial market's participants didn't want to guess. So, the markets only waited.

All markets did, not only the currency market. However, the best place to spot everything discussed here is the EURUSD daily time frame during 2016.

Until the Brexit vote in June, the pair moved gradually higher, mostly due to bears squaring the short positions (when squaring a short, the effect on the market is similar to going long).

Forex brokers, learning from the SNB (Swiss National Bank) experience (when the SNB dropped the peg on the EURCHF cross, it created chaos on the FX market, sending many brokers and traders broke in a blink of an eye) warned traders to close positions ahead of the vote.

And then the vote came, and the rest is history. The market came back to where 2016 started, and it prepared for the next significant event: the U.S. Presidential election.

Only after that, the focus shifted back to economic news and central banking. But those two events are part of fundamental analysis too.

Chapter 7

What Is a Trend and How To Ride It

A trend is a trader's friend. Everyone wants to ride it, but few know what makes a trend.

The problem with trends is that they don't form that often. And, when they do, traders tend to close a trade far too early in the process.

In this book, we already indicated that some trend indicators help traders buying dips and selling spikes in bullish or bearish trends. That's very helpful for a trend strategy when looking to add to your original position.

However, a trend's definition differs. Because financial markets spend most of the time consolidating (statistically, the currency market spends over 65% of the time in ranges), it is difficult to spot when a trend starts.

The key to a trend is to analyze how it builds the highs and lows. Thus, the series created will keep going until the trend ends.

In a bullish trend, look for the market to form a series of higher-highs and higher-lows. Until it holds, fading the trend or going short is an expensive thing to do.

Obviously, a bearish trend sees the different series forming: lower-lows and lower-highs define the bearish trend.

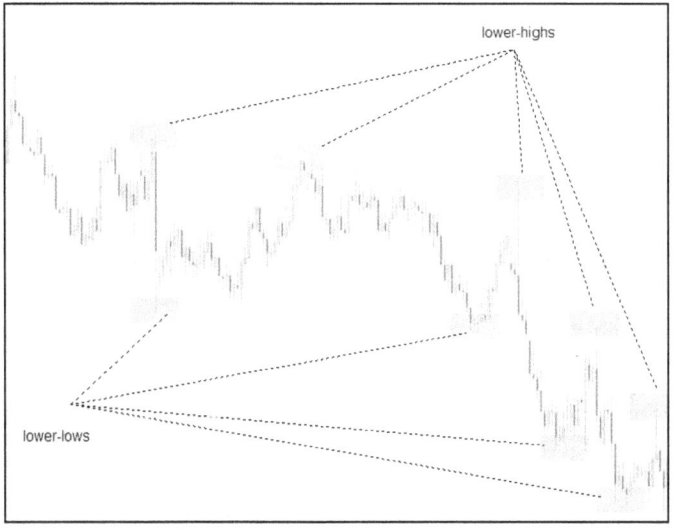

Trendlines help too. For a trendline, all you need are two points.

Traders connect the two points and then drag the resulting trendline on the right side of the chart. This way, they look for future support and resistance levels against the trendline.

But like all things technical, the break of a trendline is relative. It means that the price may break it, and the trend may still be in place. How come?

The answer comes from the very definition of a trend we mentioned earlier. A trend keeps going until the series of lower-lows and lower-highs or higher-highs, and higher-lows continues.

If the price breaks the trendline but fails to break one of the series, the trend remains valid. Just wait for a new lower-low (in a bearish trend) and higher-high (in a bullish trend) before redrawing the newly trendline.

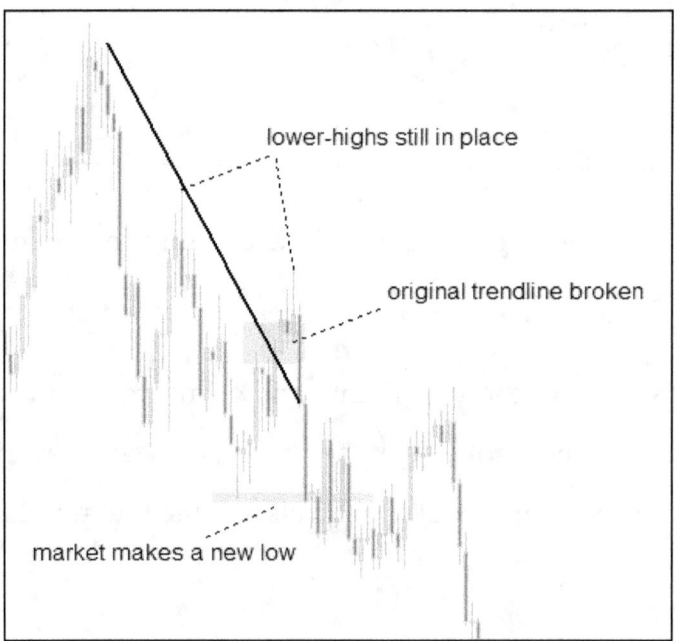

CHAPTER 8

Classic Technical Analysis Patterns To Use In Any Market

Classic technical analysis patterns belong to the Western world, namely the United States of America. Because the stock market there was one of the first places to trade financial instruments, traders looked for repetitive price action and documented the patterns.

The resulted patterns work to this day on any financial asset. As long as there is a chart, these patterns form ongoingly, on every timeframe.

Here are some of the most important classic technical analysis patterns and a basic understanding of how traders use them:

- **Head and Shoulders**. A reversal pattern, the head, and shoulders resembles the human body. It has two shoulders (left and right shoulders), a head (a spike followed by a quick retracement to the original breaking point), a neckline and a measured move. It forms both at the end of a bullish and bearish trend.

- **Wedges**. Rising and falling wedges form at the end of bullish and bearish trends. A rising wedge is falling, and a falling wedge is rising, signaling their bullishness and bearishness. Traders use numbers to count the segments of the wedge, and the resulting two trendlines give the shape of the wedge. Out of the two, the 2-4 trend line is the most important one, as it signals the wedge's break.

- **Ascending and Descending Triangles**. A triangle is a formation that acts both as a continuation and a reversal pattern. In this case, both ascending and descending triangles are continuation patterns. They revolve around a horizontal area, building energy to break higher, respectively lower. Tellingly, the price just takes its time before the previous trend resumes.

- **Flags**. Bullish and bearish flags are only continuation patterns, that can form either on the horizontal, or having a slightly downward (in the case of a bullish flag) or upward (in the case of a bearish flag) path. For this reason they are one of the most challenging patterns to trade, as sometimes what seems to be like a bullish flag turns out to be a fake pattern. Using pending orders when trading the flags helps traders avoiding being trapped on the wrong side of the market.

- **Pennants**. A pennant is still a triangle but differs than ascending and descending ones. Also called a symmetrical triangle, a pennant takes far less time until it breaks into the previous trend's direction. During a pennant's formation, the price retraces just a bit, and the consolidation takes place only because there's not enough liquidity in the market for the next leg higher. Typically, the price action before and after the pennant shows an almost vertical move.

- **Double and Triple Tops and Bottoms**. The easiest way to spot a double top or bottom is to look for the letter M, respectively the letter W on a chart. As the price hesitates around a designated level, sometimes it turns after two attempts to break higher or lower. If it tries for the third time and it fails, the market forms a triple top or bottom. A little tip here: double tops and bottoms develop more often than triple ones. And, a saying goes that triple tops and bottoms rarely hold. You choose what to make of the two statements!

Besides those mentioned above classic technical analysis patterns, some others exist too, like the cup and handle, diamond formations, rounding tops and bottoms, and so on.

However, the ones described here stood the test of time as patterns belonging to the Western approach to technical analysis that still work to this day, regardless of the market traded.

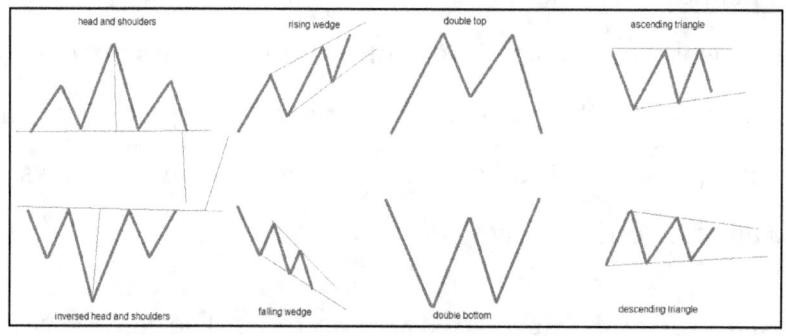

Chapter 9

Elliott Waves Theory and Why Traders Love It

Among technical trading theories, the Elliott Waves is one of the most popular among retail traders. The reason comes from the fact that is presented as a simplistic approach to markets.

However, that's only an illusion. By the time you go into details, it becomes one of the most complex trading theories every created.

Moreover, considering its rules were laid down in the middle of 1930's, when no PC existed, but everyday pen and paper charts, the findings are remarkable.

An accountant, Ralph Elliott believed that the markets represent the sum of human behavior. According to his ideas, there's no better place to see sentiments like fear or greed, pessimism, and optimism, than the market. At that time, the "playground" was the stock market.

Bound to rest at home due to sudden illness, he used the time to study price action behavior and to document stock market moves. He was quickly hooked by the findings and started to put everything together in what was to become the "secret of the universe," using his own words.

To this day, the theory has different interpretations. Elliotticians (traders that use the Elliott Waves Theory to forecast future prices) have different interpretations of the same price action.

The reason for this comes from the fact that the theory suffered many alterations in time. In a way, it is only reasonable.

It was created on the stock market before 1950's. Most of those stocks don't exist anymore.

Even the index (e.g., DJIA – Dow Jones Industrial Average) has a different componence. Not to mention that the market players changed too: today we account for more than eighty percent of the trading being automated, with trading algorithms and the high-frequency trading industry strongly influences the way prices move.

Yet, the original idea Elliott had isn't bad. In fact, it is the only one that makes sense, because of what he claimed it does:

incorporates the human nature when interpreting the market's moves.

To start with, Elliott noticed that the market forms various cycles of different degrees. And, each cycle represents an action and a reaction to the previous move.

He called them waves. More precisely, he called them impulsive and corrective waves. The action, and the reaction, or an impulsive and corrective wave that forms a market cycle.

Nowadays it is simple to spot cycles of various degrees because of the different timeframes we have on any trading platform. For example, the monthly chart corresponds to the super-cycle Elliott described, and the subsequent ones to cycles of lower degrees.

For more natural interpretation, Elliott labeled impulsive and corrective waves with numbers, respectively letters.

For impulsive waves, he found five segments to form it. Hence, the labeling is always 1-2-3-4-5.

Counting corrective waves uses letters: a-b-c for most corrective waves, a-b-c-d-e for triangles and x-waves (intervening or connecting waves) for complex corrections.

While we'll treat in more details the impulsive and corrective waves in the next books to follow, it is worth mentioning here that the theory is a logical process that doesn't leave room for error. The only way to misinterpret a market comes from either not having enough historical data to analyze it, or an error appeared.

Because of the so many cycles and rules, it is easy to make mistakes. The same complexity made it impossible for programmers to build software to automatically count waves (the ones that exist are useless!).

But one thing we know for sure is the following: the logic behind the Elliott Waves Theory considers human nature, and that is the primary driver in any market, no matter how old or young it is.

In the end, it will lead to complex and sophisticated Elliott counts that result in beautiful forecasts for any market. The one below is just an example:

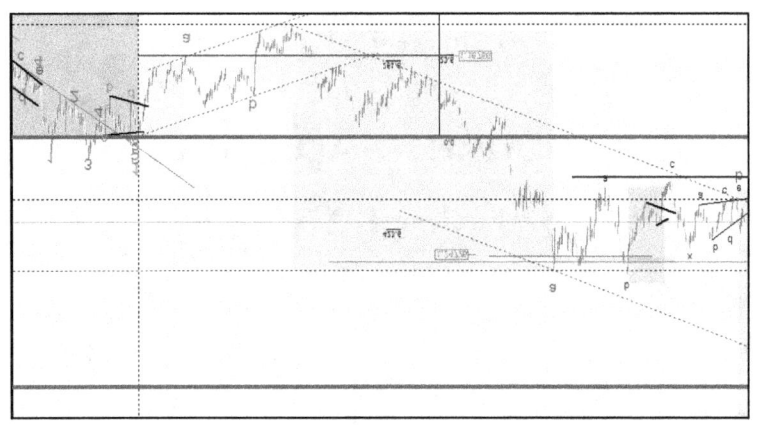

Chapter 10

The Japanese Approach To Technical Analysis

Today's technical analysis is a blend of the Western and Japanese approach. The Western world found out stunningly that the Japanese used technical analysis since early 1700.

Using candlesticks, the Japanese kept track of the movements in the rice futures, making it one of the earliest recorded technical analysis methods.

Since their introduction to the Western world, candlesticks gained impressive grounds. Nowadays, candlesticks charts are the most favored among retail traders and trading professionals alike.

A candlestick is made of two parts:

- **The real body**. This is the difference between the opening and closing prices of a candle. Either red or green, showing bearish or bullish conditions, the real body tells much about the bulk of the price action in a candle.

- **The shadows**. These are the "deviations" from the opening and closing prices. Or, in trading terms, they show the highest and lowest points in a candlestick. Hence, a candlestick has both an upper and lower shadow.

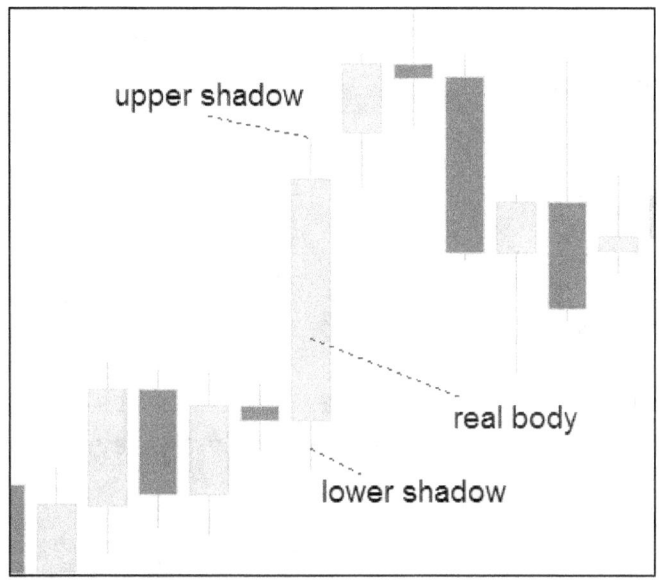

The best part of the Japanese approach to technical analysis comes from the time taken for the patterns to form. In sharp contrast with the Western patterns, the Japanese ones take far less time.

Because most of the Japanese patterns reverse a trend, the comparison is made with the Western reversal patterns, such as the head and shoulders, rising and falling wedges, double and triple tops, and so on.

Take the head and shoulders pattern for instance. The pattern takes quite some time to consolidate and reverse a trend. In the example below, the USDCAD head and shoulders pattern on the daily timeframe 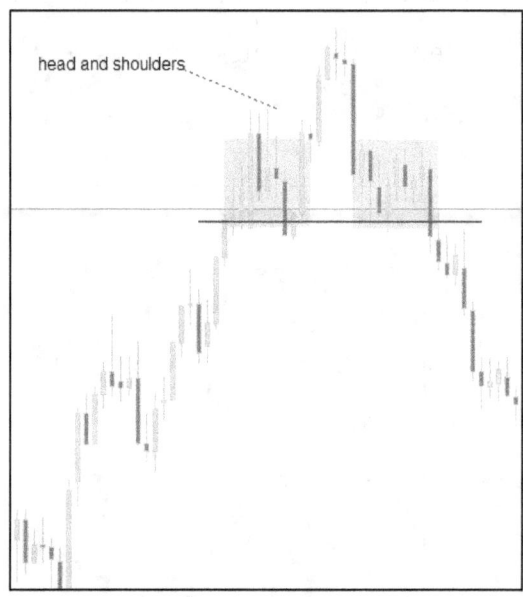 took no less than twenty-three candles to reverse a strong bullish trend. Twenty-three!

Not that is anything wrong with it, as long as traders take the right side of the market. However, what if there's some pattern that offers earlier clues about an upcoming reversal? Wouldn't you be interested in knowing more? As a trader, you would!

To the surprise of many, the Japanese patterns not only that don't take that much time, but they take far less time. Here is a list of the most powerful patterns, with more details about how to trade them in the upcoming books in the series:

- **Hammer and Shooting Star.** As the name suggested, this is a single-candle pattern that reverses a trend. The hammer forms at the bottom of a bearish trend, while the shooting star has an opposite effect: it  reverses a bearish trend. The hammer and the shooting star have a tiny real body, that might be bullish (green) or bearish (red), but a very long tail or shadow. The rule goes that the real body must fit at least two times in the shadow, for the candle to be a hammer or shooting start. Naturally, the longer the shadow, the better.

- **Bullish and Bearish Engulfing.** For the engulfing pattern, the market needs two candles. Again, the pattern forms either at the end of a bullish trend (bearish engulfing) or as the final part of a bearish trend (bullish engulfing). The first candle goes in the direction of the dominant trend, while the second one engulfs it completely. It shows reversal conditions, but there's one catch: the second candle's real body must NOT engulf the previous candle's shadow!

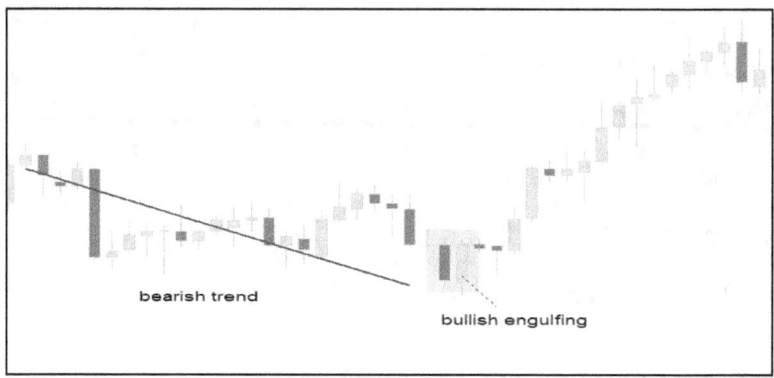

- **Morning and Evening Stars**. This time a three-candle bullish or bearish pattern, the morning or evening star is what every trader wants when looking for a reversal. They are powerful patterns, with the first candle moving in the direction of the dominant trend. Next, the candle that follows has a 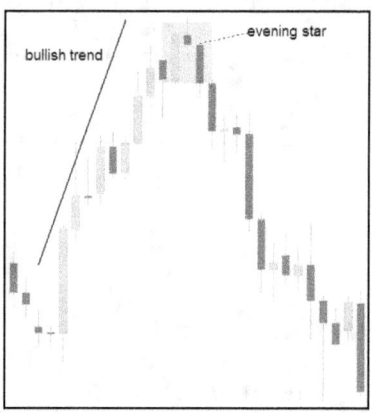 small real body, with longer shadows. Finally, the third candlestick in the pattern has a strong real body, opposite than the first candle's one, showing the new trend's direction.

- **The Doji Candle**. A one-candle pattern, the Doji candle is one of the most mysterious candles part of Japanese patterns. Because it acts both as a reversal and as a continuation pattern, it is often subject to misinterpretation. 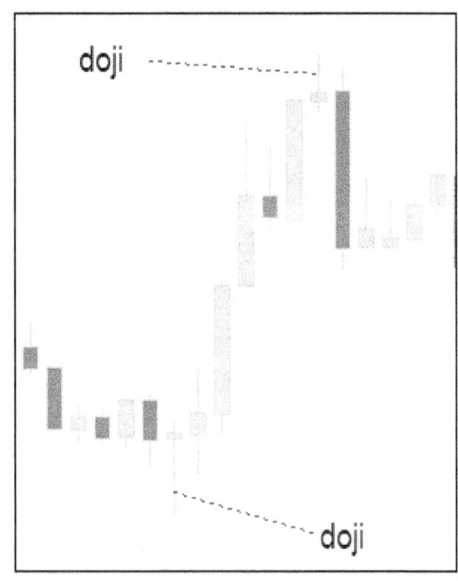 For a Doji candle to form, the market needs similar open and closing prices. However, this is a problem for the currency traders, for example, as today's execution is so accurate that most brokers show a five-digit quotation. Hence, a bit of flexibility won't hurt.

- **Piercing and Dark-Cloud Cover**. A two-candlestick pattern, the piercing and dark-cloud cover show similarities with the bullish and bearish engulfing. However, there's one difference: the second candle in the piercing or dark-cloud cover pattern doesn't engulf the previous candle's body, but minimum 50% of it. While forming more often, it is a meaningful reversal pattern that appears on all financial markets.

The candlestick patterns presented here are the most representative and powerful ones. Many others exist.

However, the aim here was to present their effectiveness in reversing a trend and the concise time needed for the patterns to complete.

Moving forward, we'll treat how to trade the patterns in next books part of our series. You'll find out that Japanese candlesticks techniques together with money management techniques, result in fabulous risk-reward ratios for a trade.

Chapter 11

The Most Important Economic News That Matters

Financial markets' volatility depends on economic news. Without volatility, the reason why the prices change, there is no room for speculation.

When the volatility index, the famous VIX, heads to lower levels for many sessions in a row, trading becomes lull, as financial markets just consolidate. As a significant driver of volatility, the economic news is essential for all markets: foreign exchange, bonds, futures, stocks, etc.

The economic calendar is free information traders can find on the Internet. It is updated all the time and shows what the main economic events for the day, week, or even weeks ahead are.

Depending on the market traded, the importance of economic news differs from trader to trader. For example, traders that focus on individual stocks may want to know the dividend date and the earnings calendar for any particular stock. That's economic news too.

On the currency market, the focus shifts on interpreting the economies present in a currency pair. Hence, traders use at general information about the state of the economy before deciding to buy or sell a currency pair.

If the trading takes place only on the U.S. stock market indices, ETF's (Exchange Traded Funds) and other related products, traders will focus mainly on the Federal Reserve of the United States monetary policy changes that affect the way indices trade.

For all categories of traders, the following economic news has the potential to move any market:

- **Inflation**. The economic term for inflation is Consumer Price Index (CPI), and it is part of every central bank's mandate. Hence, the central banks will change the interest rate level and the general monetary policy based on changes in the inflation outlook. To be one step ahead of the central banks, traders try to position themselves ahead of the central banks' decisions. A rule of thumb goes that higher inflation brings higher rates which is bullish for the currency, but bearish for stocks (excepting the financial sector).

- **Jobs Data**. Jobs are the engine for economic growth. Central banks know that and the most important central bank in the world, the Fed in the United States, has a mandate that considers job creation too. For this reason, traders carefully watch jobs data in the United States, as an indicator of how the monetary policy will change. Hence, when the NFP (Non-Farm Payrolls) in the United States comes out every first Friday of the month, the volatility on all financial markets is on the rise.

- **PMI**. The Purchasing Managers Index is a survey released in most of the capitalistic economies. It holds the key to forecasting future economic activity, and traders from all markets look at it as a benchmark to how the economy will perform. The survey's result is interpreted against the fifty value, with higher values signaling economic expansion, and lower ones, economic contraction. Typically, the PMI refers to the services and manufacturing sectors, but also to the construction one in some cases.

- **Retail Sales**. The Retail Sales indicator tells much about the state of the consumer's health. For this reason, traders closely monitor the personal expenses and disposable income evolution before concluding the future path of retail sales in an economy.

Believe it or not, but the four economic data listed above are enough for a trader's point of view. If you check the economic calendar, you'll see a plethora of economic data released every day, week and month.

However, traders use it only to prepare for what matters in financial markets: the interest rate level set by the major central banks.

Chapter 12

Central Banks and Their Role in Financial Markets

After the Nixon shock in 1971, the role of a central bank increased in importance. Slowly but surely, central banking moved from the gold standard to broad monetary policies, targeting inflation as a way to stimulate economic growth.

Today's central banking went even further. Unconventional measures (e.g., quantitative easing, long-term refinancing operations, negative interest rates, etc.) are part of the monetary policy toolkit, and the future will bring even further adjustments to what central banks can do.

Only a decade ago, expanding the balance sheet at sizes like the ones today was inconceivable. Yet, today is the norm, with major central banks holding trillions in their balance sheet.

Negative interest rates were forbidden in economic thinking. Yet, today's reality shows us major central banks in the world keep them below zero for years.

But why do central banks play a crucial role in an economy? Moreover, why do traders care?

In financial markets, regardless the market, interest rates are all that matter. But central banks are the ones that set the interest rate level. Hence, their actions dictate the price movement of any financial security.

All central banks have a mandate. Typically, the mandate refers to price stability.

As the gauge to measure price stability, inflation appears in every central bank's mandate. Studies show that economic growth picks up faster when limited inflation exists.

The economic consensus for limited inflation sits around two percent, give or take a few points. Hence, it is no wonder central banks' mandates revolve around the two percent level.

They target inflation below or close to two percent. Therefore, values like 1.8%-2.2% show moderate inflation, in line with the central banks' mandate of price stability.

Every trader knows or must know the inflation/interest rates relationship. When inflation drops below the targeted level, central banks act.

First, the communication used becomes dovish. Second, central banks will cut the interest rate. Finally, the more inflation drops, the more they'll cut and engage in easing the monetary policy.

The opposite happens when inflation exceeds the target. Central banks will raise the interest rate level to fight inflationary spirals.

There's no limit to the upside, and, until recently, the zero level was the limit to the downside. However, with negative interest rates, that limit doesn't exist anymore.

At this point in the trading series we build here, we need to explain how interest rates help stir an economy. If you  want an analogy, think of a car. In the driving seat is the central bank, and the wheel is set at 2% inflation target.

The driver turns to the left to fight lower inflation, or to the right to fight higher inflation. Each turn represents cutting or hiking the interest rate level. Or, easing and tightening the monetary policy.

A central bank is the mother of all commercial banks in an economy. It controls the money supply and supervises the economic growth.

Commercial banks face a tough decision every day. What to do with the excess liquidities?

Believe it or not, keeping money is a costly business. Why not parking them at the central bank?

How about receiving an interest in doing that?

When inflation rises, the central bank hikes the interest rate it pays to commercial banks for parking the money in overnight deposits. As such, the central bank drains liquidity from the economy, tightening the monetary conditions.

It hits the breaks. The danger of overheating grows.

When inflation drops, central banks lower the interest rate level. As such, commercial banks aren't tempted anymore to keep the money at the central bank.

Instead, commercial banks will increase their efforts to lend to businesses and population. Thus, they'll inject the much-needed liquidity in an economy that suffers.

More or less, this is the primary explanation of the fantastic relationship between inflation and interest rates.

It explains why inflation tops the list of the most important economic events to consider. And, why central banks meetings, press conferences, decisions, etc., dominate the headlines and create volatility in financial markets.

Some central banks target job creation too. The Federal Reserve of the United States (Fed) and recently the Reserve Bank of New Zealand (RBNZ) move the interest rates in such a way to stimulate job creation too.

We'll cover in greater details further aspects of modern monetary policy in the following books part of this project. At this point, keep in mind the inflation/interest rate relationship and why traders care.

Chapter 13

Market Psychology And Why Knowing Yourself Matters The Most

Traders come to markets having different expectations. Some want to make a profit as quick as possible.

Others enjoy financial markets and want to be part of the trading game. Some others invest over a more extended period, expecting moderate returns.

Regardless of the initial reason, the reality shows that traders suddenly change both the strategy and expectations after a few months of trading.

Before entering a debate as to why we need to differentiate further the purpose of trading. Most traders have a day job, which is perfectly fine.

They don't have the time to sit in front of the screens all day, plus trading is a risky business. They'll secure the income having a day job and trade after work.

While it is an approach, it doesn't fit any trading style and strategy. Most of the financial markets are open throughout the trading week, and things do happen around the clock, affecting financial markets' volatility.

So, this approach looks like treating trading more like a hobby. Again, nothing wrong with it, but it remains just that. A hobby.

Trading for a living is a different thing. Pressure mounts to make it every trading month.

After all, when trading for a living, monthly bills still come. No one gives you a break only because the markets consolidated, and you didn't make money that month. Or, several months. Or, worse, you lose some.

The danger is that only because the financial markets are open, the trader feels the need to do something. Many times, this isn't the best approach.

But what is the best approach then? The truth is that there's no recipe for it.

What works for some traders, doesn't work for others. What doesn't work for others, works for a few. And what works for a few, fails for a handful.

Introducing human nature and the so-called market psychology.

The mistake when referring to market psychology is that everyone thinks of the price changes. Wrong! Instead, the focus should be on the crowd and the individual trader.

Or, the focus should be on the trader itself. The mother of all enemies in trading is the trader itself. Yes, you, the one reading this book. You must know this before trading financial markets. You must know how to swim before jumping in the water. You must know yourself before trading financial markets.

As humans, we have great qualities. The most important one is that we're different. Variety helped our society reaching the point it reached today.

Every human being has unique emotions, feelings, hopes, dreams, and fears. There's no two alike.

But when it comes to money, most of us share the same feelings. Greed and fear resonate with most people. Hence, mastering greed and fear gives an incredible edge when trading financial markets.

That's market psychology at its best. Start with knowing yourself, master greed and fear through a disciplined approach to trading, and you'll master the markets.

Chapter 14

Introduction to Money Management

Money management or risk management or the art of managing money is the pillar of making money. The money-making business always attracted people.

To this day, there's an aura of mystery surrounding people  that are in the business of making money.

In trading, making money comes only as a result of managing risk. Hence, money management and risk management are one thing.

Before going to war, there's always a strategy. A plan B. What if something goes wrong? Do we know the way out? Is there any?

Know your way out before you go in, goes the saying. In trading, that's the stop-loss level. Or, what invalidates the original trading scenario or idea.

Many traders don't use a stop-loss for fear of seeing the market triggering it, and then reversing. They have a so-called "mental stop."

Now let me stop you right here and now. That's the first step to the margin call you'll receive soon after if you go down that path.

In case you skipped the previous chapter, do yourself a favor and reread it. Market psychology (meaning you, the trader), plays tricks on your judgment that you'll realize that only after the margin call. But then, you wished you had a stop-loss in place.

Now that we established the importance of a stop-loss order, how about the take profit?

Savvy traders don't enter a market without targeting at least two times the risk. The resulted ratio, the so-called risk-reward ratio, is 1:2. It means for the risk taken, traders target two times the reward.

Apparently, the bigger the ratio, the better. But that's the minimum. Anything below decreases the chances to survive trading financial markets. Anything above, and you get closer.

It is clear now that the pillar of money or risk management is the risk-reward ratio. Everything else comes to help to manage the trading account, to filter the wrong exposure, for example.

Things like diversification, correlations, cash position, hedging, overtrading avoidance, etc. are money management tools. But one can survive without them if the proper risk-reward ratio is in place and used for every single trade.

Chapter 15

Different Trading Styles

Earlier we mentioned that every trader has his/her personality. When facing the prospect of making or losing money, the initial trading plan almost always changes.

After some time in the markets, traders realize a few things like:

- my strategy isn't good enough to profit from all market swings
- I don't know why I trade on the five minutes chart
- why on earth did I close the trade today?
- these markets won't go anywhere, better book the profits here

Obviously, the list could go on, with human nature making traders questioning all the time what the reason why they don't make more money is? The reason, it seems, comes from market psychology.

Realizing that, is a tremendous step forward towards improved performance. Already traders know what they would like to trade most, what the perfect setup would be, what are the best days to trade, what a realistic expectation is, etc.

Moreover, they'll know where they fit in the overall process. Having said that, there are three main categories of traders:

- **Scalpers**. These guys have no patience. They like to think they can profit from every market move, and the lower timeframes are their best friends. And, for a good reason. Sophisticated scalping strategies use even the one-minute timeframe to spot a few pips move. Typically, scalpers use high volume levels to compensate for the small distance they expect the price to move. Moreover, almost all scalpers are technical traders, with few scalping of volatility created by critical economic releases. Scalpers open and multiple close trades every day, being a broker's darling, as they bring ongoing commissions for the brokerage house.

- **Swing Traders**. Looking at timeframes starting with the hourly and ending with daily, swing traders have a bigger time horizon for their trades. A trade may take a few hours or even a few weeks, and the reason may very well be fundamental, not only technical. Swing traders like to have a reason for a trade. Either technical or fundamental, the reason gives trading a logic, a sense of understanding the market. Traders in this category open and close several trades a month, mostly a couple of dozen ones. They target bigger market moves and adjust the volume accordingly.

- **Investors**. An investor has no issues with the time horizon of a trade. The only problem is the solvency. Savvy traders know a market may stay irrational for a long time. Most of the times, more than a trader stays solvent. Hence, an investors issue is not the time of a trade, but the liquidities in the trading account. The cash position is as important as an open trade, as it diminishes the opportunity cost. Investors use macroeconomics and changes in monetary policy to open a position. Their timing is not perfect, as they often are ahead of the curve and crowd. But again, that's not where the focus sits. They keep positions open even for years and use different vehicles to trade the markets, so to minimize the adjacent transaction costs (swaps, commissions, fees, interest rates, etc.)

Like it or not, every trader fits one of the three categories. Or, somewhere in between.

It may be that I, for example, trade multiple accounts. One on the bigger timeframes, one on medium ones and have a scalping strategy. I'm a bit of everything into one.

But that's rare. The bulk of traders fit into one of the three. Which one are you? I'm sure that by the time you ended up reading this chapter, you know for sure where you fit.

Besides the trading styles mentioned here, the market moves more and more influenced by trading algorithms or robots. With super-computers dominating our everyday lives, it is no wonder they dominate financial markets too.

However, even high-frequency trading follows the same rules. Money management, market psychology, and even the trading styles fit the industry too.

The next book of our series will introduce to you the amazing currency market. Full of opportunities, Forex trading, changed the way individuals dream about success in life.

Are you one of them? Read and find out!

www.ingramcontent.com/pod-product-compliance
Lightning Source LLC
Chambersburg PA
CBHW052339220526
45472CB00001B/492